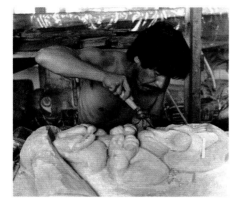

Carving a Totem Pole

TEXT AND PHOTOGRAPHS BY **VICKIE JENSEN**

FOREWORD BY **NORMAN TAIT**

HENRY HOLT AND COMPANY
NEW YORK

*Carving a Totem Pole is for Norman Tait,
Robert "Chip" Tait, Isaac Tait, Harry "Hammy" Martin,
Wayne Young, and their families. Their goodwill, knowledge,
and friendship continue to shape my work.
This book is also dedicated to my sons, Nels and Luke.*

Henry Holt and Company, Inc.
Publishers since 1866
115 West 18th Street
New York, New York 10011

Henry Holt is a registered
trademark of Henry Holt and Company, Inc.

First published in the United States in 1996 by Henry Holt and Company, Inc.
Originally published in Canada in 1994 by Douglas & McIntyre Ltd.

Library of Congress Cataloging-in-Publication Data
Jensen, Vicki.
    Carving a totem pole / text and photographs by Vicki Jensen.
        Summary: Describes how Nisga'a artist Norman Tait designs
    and carves a totem pole, trains his relatives to carve,
    and participates in the pole-raising ceremonies.
        1. Totem poles—British Columbia—Juvenile literature.   2. Niska
    wood-carving—British Columbia—Juvenile literature.   3. Niska
    Indians—Rites and ceremonies—Juvenile literature.   [1. Totem
    poles.   2. Niska Indians—Rites and ceremonies.   3. Indians of North
    America—British Columbia—Rites and ceremonies.]   I. Title.
    E98.T65J45   1995   730'.89'974—dc20   95-19941

ISBN 0-8050-3754-3

First American Edition—1996

Printed in the United States of America on acid-free paper. ∞
10 9 8 7 6 5 4 3 2 1

FOREWORD

Before our history was ever written down, the old people kept all the knowledge in their heads. They were the only "books" that there were. They used totem poles to teach us about the past. It was important to them that the children know their ancestors at an early age because they, too, would become the history books of our people.

The elders would take children aside and tell them a story. The next day they'd tell it to them again. The elders told their legends over and over. When I was a child, I used to sit with my uncle and listen to his stories. This is the way that I learned about my family history.

I hope this book will help children understand the importance of the totem pole. I want them to know that poles helped our people to learn our family history for generations and generations, all the way back to mythical times.

When a totem pole is raised, it is like the birth of an important person. The pole is given a name and treated with the same kind of respect you would give a chief. Like the elders, each pole is a teacher, a storyteller.

The pictures and words in *Carving a Totem Pole* say that native people are alive. Our Nisga'a culture is alive. Our art is alive. This book and the totem pole we carved tell that story.

Norman Tait
Nisga'a Artist

No one knows who carved the first totem pole. But totem poles were already standing in native villages when European explorers came to the Northwest Coast of Canada more than two hundred years ago. The explorers wondered about these towering wooden carvings and tried to draw pictures of them in their journals.

Those early poles must have taken a very long time to carve, since there was no hard metal for adzes, chisels, or knives. In those days, carvers made blades out of sharpened clam and mussel shell, stone or bone. When trading began with explorers, the people eagerly traded their sea otter pelts for iron tools. Many chiefs became wealthy from this trading and were able to pay master carvers to design poles for them—poles that told the old stories of their noble families. By the mid-1860s, some villages had more than seventy poles.

But trading brought other changes, too. Thousands of people died from the new diseases, alcohol, and firearms that Europeans brought to native villages. Missionaries came, preaching that Christianity was superior to the old beliefs. Many of the people were convinced, and they stopped their traditional ways of feasting, singing, and dancing with ceremonial regalia. Native children were sent away to boarding schools, where they were forbidden to speak their languages. Laws were passed prohibiting the important ceremonial events called pot-latches. Few new totem poles were raised, and knowledge of how to carve them was nearly lost. The rich native cultures of the Northwest Coast seemed to be dying out.

Over the next hundred years only a handful of people continued to carve and teach others. Then in the 1950s, when it was almost too late, two museums in British Columbia began projects to restore old poles and carve new ones. They hired the last of the master carvers, and these carvers trained apprentices. Slowly the wealth of ceremonial masks, rattles, feast dishes, and totem poles was built up again. Today, Northwest Coast art is recognized all over the world and, once again, there are many carvers.

Carving a Totem Pole is the story of how Nisg̲a'a artist Norman Tait carves a modern totem pole. It is also the story of how he trains relatives such as his son, nephew, and cousin, and how his large family helps with the ceremonies that are an important part of raising a new totem pole.

In the early days, a carver would search for a long time to find the best cedar tree for his next totem pole. The tree had to be very large, with no rot or twists in the wood and few limbs growing off the side he would carve. Today, many old forests in British Columbia are being cut down to make lumber, paper, and other wood products, so it is even more difficult to find a cedar that has been growing for hundreds of years. Carvers still feel such trees are very special, and they often thank the cedar for giving up its life to become a totem pole.

Once a suitable cedar tree is found and cut down, the back is sliced off. This massive log will become a doorway totem pole for the Native Education Centre in Vancouver, British Columbia (the extra slab at the base of the pole will fit into the doorway). Nisg̲a'a artist Norman Tait has been hired to design and carve the pole. Like carvers in the old days, he relies on family members for his crew. Norman's youngest brother, Robert "Chip" Tait, will be the foreman. He is the boss of the other carvers. Another crew member is Harry "Hammy" Martin, a cousin. He has done some carving, but this will be his first large pole. Norman's son, Isaac Tait, and his nephew, Wayne Young, are the apprentices who are just learning how to carve. The crew has three months to carve the forty-two-foot pole.

After the back has been sliced off, the log is hollowed out so it will dry evenly and not split. Then the crew members roll the mighty log over and strip off the bark.

Now they start to shape the log by cutting away the outer sap wood. The carvers want to get down to the inner heart wood, making a log that is smooth and evenly rounded, with no bumps. They use traditional, well-sharpened tools, called adzes, that they have made themselves. Adzing is hard work. The young apprentices have sore muscles and blisters by the end of each day.

When he is ready to start cutting the doorway at the base of the pole, Chip draws the outline of the door on the wood. Then he climbs up on the log and checks to see if the door will be tall enough. He fits!

Chip chooses a long-bladed chain saw and cuts deep into the log. He could use an adze to remove the wood, but the job would take much longer. A chain saw is a handy shortcut.

Eventually, the pole is moved inside a carving shed at the University of British Columbia. There the crew can work long hours, even when it is raining outside. Now that the log is smooth and round, Norman can begin the actual carving of the pole. So far only the doorway has been started at the butt end of the log.

In the past, there were many different kinds of totem poles. Some were carved in memory of a chief's death. Others supported the massive beams of a house. Some held the remains of a dead chief or were grave markers. A few were giant figures set up at the beach to welcome visitors. Male and female chiefs had poles made that told the mythic stories of their families. The characters of these stories were carved onto the pole, including the family's crests, or spiritual ancestors. Today, some totem poles are carved for museums, shopping malls, businesses, or education centres. None of them have family stories or crests, so Norman has chosen a story of his own to use on this pole.

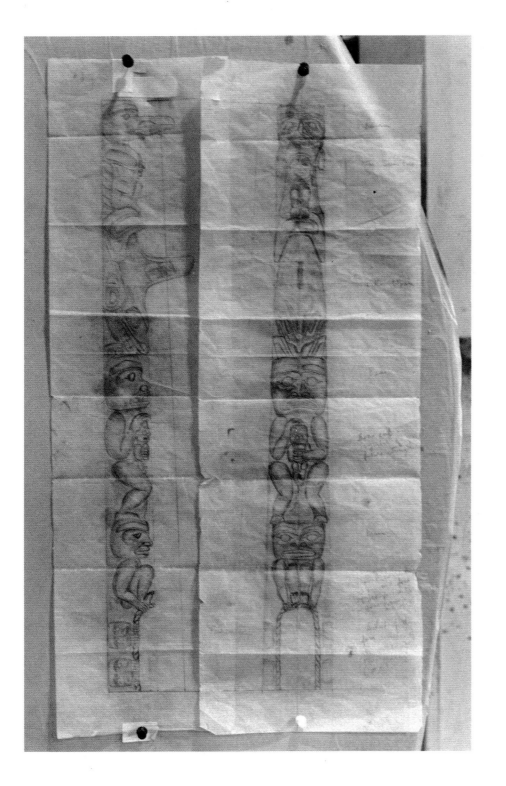

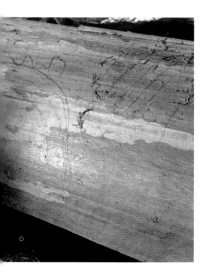

Norman's design is based on a story about how people learned to live in harmony with the creatures of the sea, sky, and land. He has put Raven at the top of the pole, followed by Killerwhale, then Bear, and finally Man crouched over the doorway. He has also added a Moon figure between Raven's wings and has Bear holding a little Wolf cub. Around the doorway are four small human faces.

Working from drawings, Norman and Chip measure approximately how high each figure will be on the pole. Then Norman begins sketching Raven's face and wings, as well as the Moon figure. He draws freely, not worrying about where the exact lines will go. Later he pencils in darker, more definite outlines.

Finally, he prepares a full-size paper drawing of each of the remaining figures for other crew members to trace onto the wood. These tracings serve as guidelines and help Norman judge the exact size and placement of the figures.

Norman is impatient to begin cutting the first figures. He starts at the top of the pole, shaping Raven's forehead. Then, while crew members are still tracing the lower creatures, he begins shaping the legs of the Moon figure and Raven's wings. He alternates using his big adze, axe, and chain saw, seeing in his mind how deeply to cut. Chunks of wood fly off the pole. Norman calls these first cuts an explosion, and they feel like one!

There are two pieces of this totem pole that must be carved from separate blocks of wood and added on later—Whale's fin and Raven's beak. Norman gives the young apprentices the responsibility of carving these pieces. He assigns the beak to Isaac. Wayne will do the fin.

Norman, Chip, and Hammy rough-cut the rest of the figures. Then Chip demonstrates how to use a mallet and chisel to define each creature from the background wood. At this point, all the arms, legs, and heads look square and chunky.

The next stage in carving the totem pole is rounding the figures and sculpting the faces. Isaac's strong adze strokes take the sharp edges off Bear's legs and arms. He is careful not to cut too deeply where Norman has drawn small circles on the wood. These mark the areas that will become the wristbones and anklebones that are a trademark of Norman's carving.

Chip puts his hands over the eyeballs, feeling whether or not they are equally shaped. The carvers learn how to measure with their hands as well as with their eyes. "Your hands will tell you if one side is higher," he explains, "but you need to practice."

Each of the crew members will carve one of the four faces around the doorway all by himself. Norman calls these faces signature pieces, because they are a way of signing each carver's name to the totem pole. After the faces have been drawn on the wood, the carvers begin rough-cutting with smaller, single-handed adzes. Although the faces are all drawn from the same outline, they soon look quite different from one another.

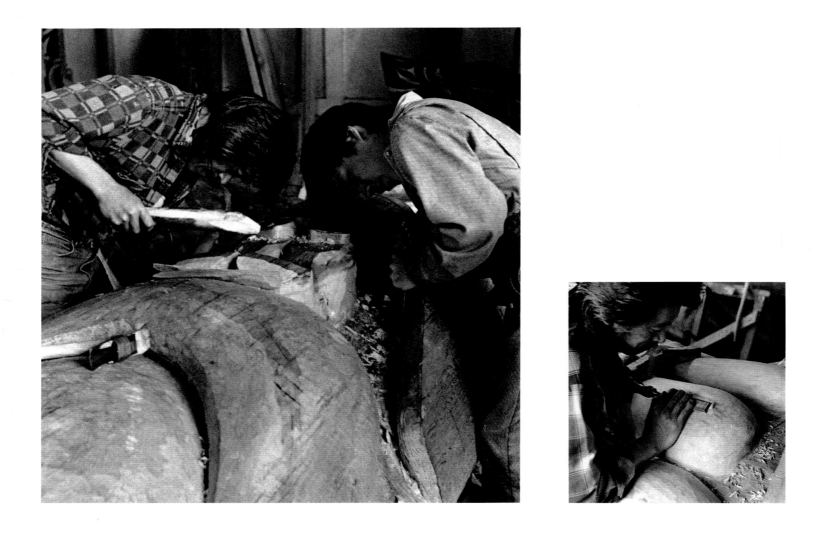

Working head to head, Hammy and Isaac use mallets and chisels to carve hollows under Raven's big wings. "This undercutting puts a shadow under it and gives it a bit more life," Chip explains.

Hammy's wide chisel puts a smooth finish on Man's legs. Carvers can also use a curved knife to make hundreds of tiny cuts that blend together for a textured finish. Sandpaper is never used on a totem pole.

Now the fin looks slim and streamlined. But Norman points out that the base of the fin is still too thick. It needs to be cut down more. He wants it to flow naturally out of the body of Whale. When the fin and beak are completely finished, they will be attached to the pole with waterproof glue and wooden pins, called dowels.

On this pole, Norman's signature piece is Wolf cub. It represents his youngest son, Micah, who is Wolf clan. Norman is a high-ranking Eagle clan chief. But among the Nisg̲a'a, each child inherits his or her clan identity from the mother.

Nearly complete, this Wolf cub has chubby feet, curled hands, and an impish smile.

For finer work, the carvers switch to different tools. They use knives with straightedged and curved blades that they have made themselves. Norman wants this totem pole to age naturally to a soft gray. So rather than paint it, crew members use their knives to cut V-shaped grooves around the eyes, eyebrows, and nostrils of each figure. These grooves, rather than color, highlight the figures.

Finally, after three months of learning and labor, the pole is done. "For us, carving a totem pole was just work, until we all stood back and looked at it," Chip explains. "Then everybody felt the same way. Wow, what a beautiful pole!"

It's time to move the completed pole to the Native Education Centre where it will be raised. The totem pole is as tall as eight men standing on each other's shoulders. And it is very heavy! Friends are invited to help carry the massive work of art. The crew members put on the ceremonial tunics and leggings that the family women have sewn for the pole raising. Norman wears his deerskin shirt and dance apron. He and Chip use drum signals to tell the carriers when to lift and how far to go.

Finally the totem pole is carefully loaded onto a long truck.

When the truck rolls up to the new building, the carvers and other family members welcome the pole with a Nisga'a song. Norman feels that a totem pole is a powerful storyteller and must be shown the same respect as a great chief.

The next day is the pole raising. Tait family members and other Nisga'a arrive early. All of them bring button blankets and other ceremonial items such as frontlets, rattles, and talking sticks. Although Norman's mind is full of details about the difficult pole raising, he still takes time to give his niece a reassuring hug.

Nowadays, some totem poles are quickly lifted into position using cranes. But Norman wants his pole raised in the traditional way. Hundreds of well-wishers, friends, and students from the Native Education Centre will pull up this totem pole by hand. They will use only ropes and pulleys, so it is important that the thick ropes be positioned properly.

Before the pole can be pulled upright, it must be carefully rolled over onto its side. Norman leaps up onto the pole. He drums out a signal to tighten the ropes and begin the turn.

Crowds of people pull on each of the lines. Slowly, slowly, the pole inches skyward. The ropes creak and strain under the weight.

With a last push at the base, the massive totem pole finally slides into position. The crowd explodes with cheers and whistles. Grinning with joy, Hammy and Isaac hug each other.

Chip recalls, "When I looked up at the pole, I felt just like crying. I couldn't believe it!"

With the pole safely raised, the ceremonies begin. Norman puts on his button blanket and a finely carved eagle helmet. He drums as his mother sings a welcoming song for the pole. Finally, clutching a handful of eagle feathers, Norman dances.

The members of the crew stand proud in their regalia. Looking at them, Norman says, "I feel like I just brought up a whole family of kids, and now they're men."

Norman tells the story of the pole to the hundreds of people who have helped raise it. Then Wolf clan chief Mercy Robinson Thomas officially names the pole. She calls out the Nisg̲a'a name, Wil Sayt Bakwhlgat, three times. The name means "the place where the people gather."

After speeches and a feast of deer stew, the crowd begins to leave. The carvers gather with their families at the base of the pole for photos. They want to remember this day always.

The director of the Native Education Centre explains that the building would have been cheaper to build without the pole. But then it would have looked like any other place. This totem pole says, "We're here! Native people are alive!"

A plaque next to the totem pole reads,
"This pole is dedicated to all Indian people who have gone on before, to those who currently struggle for our survival, and to the generations yet unborn."